D0487561

Born to Shop®

B²S Born to Shop®

In Praise of the Modern Woman

SEVENOAKS

First published in Great Britain in 2006 by Sevenoaks
20 Mortimer Street
London W1T 3JW

Born to Shop © and ® 2006 History and Heraldry Ltd

This book is sold subject to the condition that it shall
not, by way of trade or otherwise, be lent, resold, hired out
or otherwise circulated without the publisher's prior written
consent in any form of binding or cover other than that in
which it is published and without a similar condition including
this condition, being imposed on the subsequent purchaser.

All rights reserved.

ISBN: 978-1-86200-380-4

Printed in Dubai

Contents

Born to be Beautiful

Lord if you won't make me skinny, please make my friends fat

I keep trying to lose weight, but it keeps finding me

Whenever I get the urge to exercise, I lie down until the feeling passes

Warning: This person may contain coarse language, and occasional scenes of nudity

I am usually gorgeous,
but it's my day off

At my age a soak
in the tub is just a
wild night in

You can't control everything, your hair was put on your head to remind you of that

Born to be the Model Partner

Sometimes I wake
up grumpy, and
sometimes I let
him sleep

I don't do mornings

Don't try to understand
me, just love me

I'm in my own world.
It's ok, they know
me here

If at first you
don't succeed,
try it your wife's way

All men are created equal, equally useless

When I married
Mr Right, I didn't
know his first name
was always

Laugh, and the world
laughs with you...

...snore and you sleep alone

Would you like to speak
to the man in charge or
the woman who knows
what's happening

When I said
'I do', I didn't
mean everything

B.B.Q. – (bar-by-que) –

compact home incinerator

used for disposing of bulky

pieces of meat and poultry

A real man can barbie
any time, anywhere

I can only please one
person per day.
Today is not your day.
Tomorrow doesn't look
very good either

Three things real men
can't say, I'm wrong,
I'm lost, I can't fix it

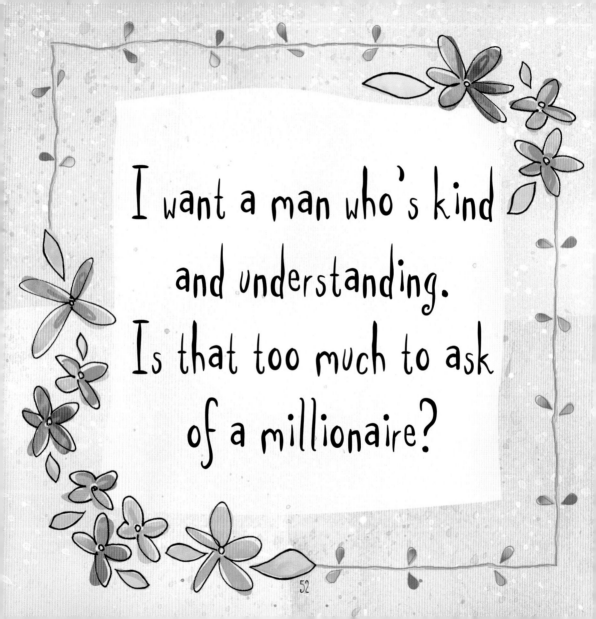

I want a man who's kind
and understanding.
Is that too much to ask
of a millionaire?

Born to Eat What you Can

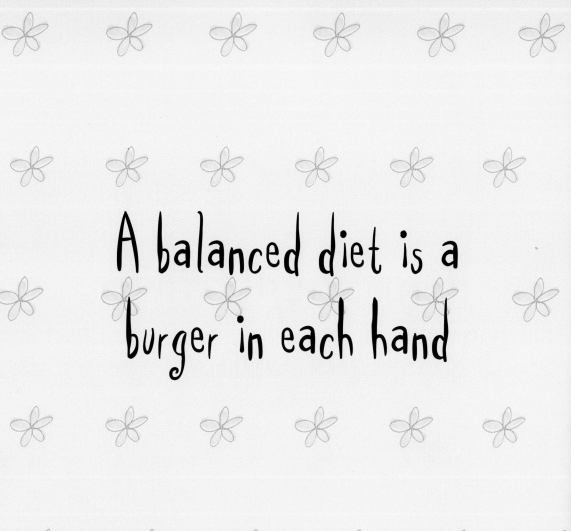

A balanced diet is a burger in each hand

Never eat more than
you can lift

Save the Earth,
it's the only planet
with chocolate

There's nothing better
than a good friend
except a good friend
with chocolate

At Easter, size does count

So much chocolate
log, so little time

Born to be a
Yummy Mummy

We child proofed the
house, but they keep
finding their way in

Welcome to Grandma's house. Children spoilt while you wait

Mothers of little
boys work from son
up to son down

'M' is for Mother, not for Maid

If a mother's place is
in the home, why am I
always in the car!

Born to be Wild

Seen it all, done it all, can't remember most of it

One tequila,
two tequila, three
tequila, floor!

I'm on a gin and tonic diet, so far I've lost two days

Life's too short to
drink bad wine

The whole world is about
three drinks behind

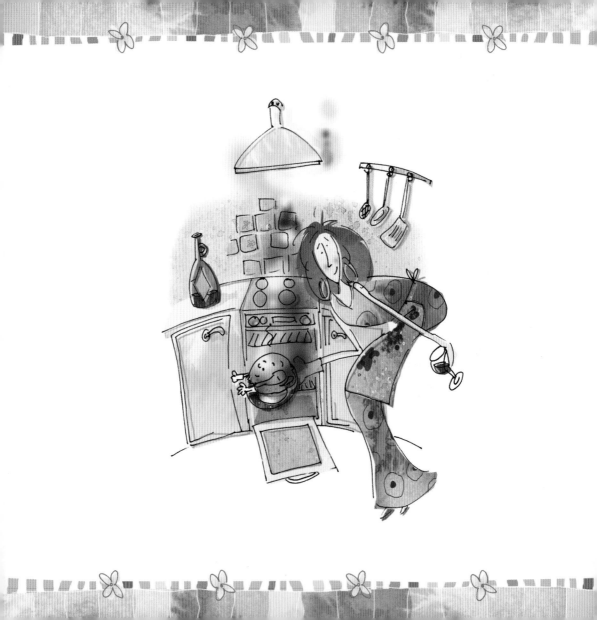

Born to be a Domestic Goddess

I kiss better than I cook

I love to cook with wine,
sometimes I even put it
in the food

Tis the season to be jolly

It's all too much, wake
me when it's over

Too much of a good
thing is wonderful

I am woman
I am invincible
I am tired

You can touch the
dust, but please
don't write in it

Many people have eaten in this kitchen and have gone on to live normal healthy lives

If you want breakfast in bed,
sleep in the kitchen

We eat all the main food groups — microwave, fast and frozen

If you want the best
seat in the house,
you'll have to move
the cat

People who don't like cats must have been mice in a previous life

Love endures all things

Born to Succeed

No coffee, no workee

We may not have it
all together...
but together we
have it all

Hard work pays off
in the future, laziness
pays off now

Instant human, just add bubbles

This life must be a test,
if it were the real thing we'd
be given better instructions

I don't suffer from stress,
but I am a carrier

Good morning...
let the stress begin

Born to be Part of the Gang

You can't have
too many friends,
or pairs of shoes

Friends like you
don't grow on trees.
I know this is true,
but if friends were flowers
there is no doubt how
quickly I'd pick you

For listening and caring and giving and sharing, for always being there thank you

Precious and few are
friends like you

A hug is a great gift one size fits all

Friends are the family we choose for ourselves

There are special people
who touch our lives in a
certain way and having
known them we will never
be the same again

I can't imagine in all the world a better friend than you

Today I stopped and thought, what a special friend I have in you

Friends bring out the beautiful things in each other that nobody else looks hard enough to find

You'll always be my friend, you know too much